The Leverage Effect:

How Warren Buffett Achieves Market Alpha

Maxwell Stark

Berkshire Hathaway has realized a Sharpe ratio of 0.76, higher than any other stock or mutual fund with a history of more than 30 years, and Berkshire has a significant alpha to traditional risk factors. However, we find that the alpha becomes insignificant when controlling for exposures to Betting-Against-Beta and Quality-Minus-Junk factors. Further, we estimate that Buffett's leverage is about 1.6-to-1 on average. Buffett's returns appear to be neither luck nor magic, but, rather, reward for the use of leverage combined with a focus on cheap, safe, quality stocks. Decomposing Berkshires' portfolio into ownership in publicly traded stocks versus wholly-owned private companies, we find that the former performs the best, suggesting that Buffett's returns are more due to stock selection than to his effect on management. These results have broad implications for market efficiency and the implementability of academic factors.

1. Introduction: Understanding the Oracle's Alpha

While much has been said and written about Warren Buffett and his investment style, there has been little rigorous empirical analysis that explains his performance. Every investor has a view on how Buffett has done it, but we seek the answer via a thorough empirical analysis in light of some the latest research on the drivers of returns.[1]

Buffett's success has become the focal point of the debate on market efficiency that continues to be at the heart of financial economics. Efficient market academics suggest that his success may simply be luck, the happy winner of a coin-flipping contest as articulated by Michael Jensen at a famous 1984 conference at Columbia Business School celebrating the 50th anniversary of the book by Graham and Dodd (1934).[2] Tests of this argument via a statistical analysis of the extremity of Buffett's performance cannot fully resolve the issue. Instead, Buffett countered at the conference that it is no coincidence that many of the winners in the stock market come from the same intellectual village, "Graham-and-Doddsville" (Buffett (1984)). How can Buffett's argument be tested? Ex post selecting successful investors who are informally classified to belong to Graham-and-Doddsville is subject to biases. We rigorously examine this argument using a different strategy. We show that Buffett's performance can be largely explained by exposures to value, low-risk, and quality factors. This finding is consistent with the idea

---

[1] Based on the original insights of Black (1972) and Black, Jensen, and Scholes (1972), Frazzini and Pedersen (2013) show that leverage and margin requirements change equilibrium risk premia. They show that investors without binding leverage constraints can profit from Betting Against Beta (BAB), buying low-risk assets and shorting risky assets. Frazzini and Pedersen (2012) extend this finding to derivatives with embedded leverage, Asness, Frazzini, and Pedersen (2012a) to the risk-return relation across asset classes. Asness, Frazzini, and Pedersen (2013) consider fundamental measures of risk and other accounting based measures of "quality," i.e., characteristics that make a company more valuable.

[2] The book by Graham and Dodd (1934) is credited with laying the foundation for investing based on value and quality, and Graham and Dodd were Buffett's professors at Columbia.

that investors from Graham-and-Doddsville follow similar strategies to achieve similar results and inconsistent with stocks being chosen based on coin flips. Hence, Buffett's success appears not to be luck. Rather, Buffett personalizes the success of value and quality investment, providing out-of-sample evidence on the ideas of Graham and Dodd (1934). The fact that both aspects of Graham and Dodd (1934) investing – value and quality – predict returns[3] is consistent with their hypothesis of limited market efficiency. However, one might wonder whether such factor returns can be achieved by any real life investor after transaction costs and funding costs? The answer appears to be a clear "yes" based on Buffett's performance and our decomposition of it.

Buffett's record is remarkable in many ways, but just how spectacular has the performance of Berkshire Hathaway been compared to other stocks or mutual funds? Looking at all U.S. stocks from 1926 to 2011 that have been traded for more than 30 years, we find that Berkshire Hathaway has the highest Sharpe ratio among all. Similarly, Buffett has a higher Sharpe ratio than all U.S. mutual funds that have been around for more than 30 years.

So how large is this Sharpe ratio that has made Buffett one of the richest people in the world? We find that the Sharpe ratio of Berkshire Hathaway is 0.76 over the period 1976-2011. While nearly double the Sharpe ratio of the overall stock market, this is lower than many investors imagine. Adjusting for the market exposure, Buffett's information

---

[3] Value stocks on average outperform growth stocks as documented by Stattman (1980), Rosenberg, Reid, and Lanstein (1985), and Fama and French (1992) and high-quality stocks outperform junk stocks on average as documented by Asness, Frazzini, and Pedersen (2013) and references therein.

ratio[4] is even lower, 0.66. This Sharpe ratio reflects high average returns, but also significant risk and periods of losses and significant drawdowns.

If his Sharpe ratio is very good but not super-human, then how did Buffett become among the richest in the world? The answer is that Buffett has boosted his returns by using leverage, and that he has stuck to a good strategy for a very long time period, surviving rough periods where others might have been forced into a fire sale or a career shift. We estimate that Buffett applies a leverage of about 1.6-to-1, boosting both his risk and excess return in that proportion. Thus, his many accomplishments include having the conviction, wherewithal, and skill to operate with leverage and significant risk over a number of decades.

This leaves the key question: How does Buffett pick stocks to achieve this attractive return stream that can be leveraged? We identify several general features of his portfolio: He buys stocks that are "safe" (with low beta and low volatility), "cheap" (i.e., value stocks with low price-to-book ratios), and high-quality (meaning stocks that profitable, stable, growing, and with high payout ratios). This statistical finding is certainly consistent with Graham and Dodd (1934) and Buffett's writings, e.g.:

> *Whether we're talking about socks or stocks, I like buying quality merchandise when it is marked down*
>
> *– Warren Buffett, Berkshire Hathaway Inc., Annual Report, 2008.*

---

[4] The Information ratio is defined as the intercept in a regression of monthly excess returns divided by the standard deviation of the residuals. The explanatory variable in the regression is the monthly excess returns of the CRSP value-weighted market portfolio. Sharpe ratios and information ratios are annualized.

Interestingly, stocks with these characteristics – low risk, cheap, and high quality – tend to perform well in general, not just the ones that Buffett buys. Hence, perhaps these characteristics can explain Buffett's investment? Or, is his performance driven by an idiosyncratic Buffett skill that cannot be quantified?

The standard academic factors that capture the market, size, value, and momentum premia cannot explain Buffett's performance so his success has to date been a mystery (Martin and Puthenpurackal (2008)). Given Buffett's tendency to buy stocks with low return risk and low fundamental risk, we further adjust his performance for the Betting-Against-Beta (BAB) factor of Frazzini and Pedersen (2013) and the Quality Minus Junk (QMJ) factor of Asness, Frazzini, and Pedersen (2013). We find that accounting for these factors explains a large part of Buffett's performance. In other words, accounting for the general tendency of high-quality, safe, and cheap stocks to outperform can explain much of Buffett's performance and controlling for these factors makes Buffett's alpha statistically insignificant.

To illustrate this point in a different way, we create a portfolio that tracks Buffett's market exposure and active stock-selection themes, leveraged to the same active risk as Berkshire. We find that this systematic Buffett-style portfolio performs comparably to Berkshire Hathaway. Buffett's genius thus appears to be at least partly in recognizing early on, implicitly or explicitly, that these factors work, applying leverage without ever having to fire sale, and sticking to his principles. Perhaps this is what he means by his modest comment:

Ben Graham taught me 45 years ago that in investing it is not

necessary to do extraordinary things to get extraordinary results

However, it cannot be emphasized enough that explaining Buffett's performance with the benefit of hindsight does not diminish his outstanding accomplishment. He decided to invest based on these principles half a century ago. He found a way to apply leverage. Finally, he managed to stick to his principles and continue operating at high risk even after experiencing some ups and downs that have caused many other investors to rethink and retreat from their original strategies.

Finally, we consider whether Buffett's skill is due to his ability to buy the right stocks versus his ability as a CEO. Said differently, is Buffett mainly an investor or a manager? To address this, we decompose Berkshire's returns into a part due to investments in publicly traded stocks and another part due to private companies run within Berkshire. The idea is that the return of the public stocks is mainly driven by Buffett's stock selection skill, whereas the private companies could also have a larger element of management. We find that both public and private companies contribute to Buffett's performance, but the portfolio of public stocks performs the best, suggesting that Buffett's skill is mostly in stock selection. Why then does Buffett rely heavily on private companies as well, including insurance and reinsurance businesses? One reason might be that this structure provides a steady source of financing, allowing him to leverage his stock selection ability. Indeed, we find that 36% of Buffett's liabilities consist of insurance float with an average cost below the T-Bill rate.

In summary, we find that Buffett has developed a unique access to leverage that he has invested in safe, high-quality, cheap stocks and that these key characteristics can largely explain his impressive performance. Buffett's unique access to leverage is consistent with the idea that he can earn BAB returns driven by other investors' leverage constraints. Further, both value and quality predict returns and both are needed to explain Buffett's performance. Buffett's performance appears not to be luck, but an expression that value and quality investing can be implemented in an actual portfolio (although, of course, not by all investors who must collectively hold the market).

2. Data Sources

Our data comes from several sources. We use stock return data from the CRSP database, balance sheet data from the Compustat/XpressFeed database as well as hand-collected annual reports, holdings data for Berkshire Hathaway from Thomson Financial Institutional (13F) Holding Database (based on Berkshire's SEC filings), the size and cost of the insurance float from hand-collected comments in Berkshire Hathaway's annual reports, and mutual fund data from the CRSP Mutual Fund Database. We also use factor returns from Ken French's website and from Frazzini and Pedersen (2013) and Asness, Frazzini, and Pedersen (2013). We describe our data sources and data filters in more detail in Appendix B.

3. Buffett's Track Record

Buffett's track record is clearly outstanding. A dollar invested in Berkshire Hathaway in November 1976 (when our data sample starts) would have been worth more than $1500 at the end of 2011. Over this time period, Berkshire realized an average annual return of 19.0% in excess of the T-Bill rate, significantly outperforming the general stock market's average excess return of 6.1%.

Berkshire stock also entailed more risk, realized a volatility of 24.9%, higher than the market volatility of 15.8%. However, Berskhire's excess return was high even relative to its risk, earning a Sharpe ratio of 19.0%/24.9% = 0.76, nearly twice the market's Sharpe ratio of 0.39. Berkshire realized a market beta of only 0.7, an important point that we will discuss in more detail when we analyze the types of stocks that Buffett buys. Adjusting Berkshire's performance for market exposure, we compute its Information ratio to be 0.66.

These performance measures reflect Buffett's impressive returns, but also that Berkshire has been associated with some risk. Berkshire has had a number of down years and drawdown periods. For example, from June 30, 1998 to February 29, 2000, Berkshire lost 44% of its market value while the overall stock market gained 32%. While many fund managers might have had trouble surviving such a shortfall of 76%, Buffett's impeccable reputation and unique structure as a corporation allowed him to stay the course and rebound as the internet bubble burst.

To put Buffett's performance in perspective, we compare Berkshire's Sharpe and Information ratios to those of all other U.S. common stocks. If Buffett is more of a stock picker than a manager, an even better reference group than other stocks might be the universe of actively managed mutual funds so Table 1 compares Berkshire to both of these groups.

Buffett is in the top 3% among all mutual funds and top 7% among all stocks. However, the stocks or mutual funds with the highest Sharpe ratios are often ones that have only existed for a short time periods and had a good run, which is associated with a large degree of randomness.

To minimize the effect of randomness, Table 1 also compares Berkshire to all stocks or mutual funds with at least a 10-year or 30-year history. Buffett's performance is truly outstanding seen in this perspective. Among all stocks with at least a 30-year history from 1926 to 2011, Berkshire has realized the highest Sharpe ratio and Information ratio. If you could travel back in time and pick one stock in 1976, Berkshire would be your pick. Figures 1 and 2 also illustrate how Buffett lies in the very best tail of the performance distribution of mutual funds and stocks that have survived at least 30 years.

4. Buffett's Leverage

Buffett's large returns come both from his high Sharpe ratio and his ability to leverage his performance to achieve large returns at higher risk. Buffett uses leverage to magnify returns, but how much leverage does he use? Further, what are Buffett's sources of leverage, their terms, and costs? To answer these questions, we study Berkshire Hathaway's balance sheet, which can be summarized as follows:

Stylized Balance Sheet of Berkshire Hathaway

Assets	Liabilities and shareholders' equity
Publicly traded equities	Liabilities
Privately held companies	Equity
Cash	
Total assets	Total liabilities

We can compute Buffett's leverage (L) as follows:

$$L_t = \frac{TA_t^{MV} - Cash_t^{MV}}{Equity_t^{MV}}$$

This measure of leverage is computed each month as Berkshire's total assets (TA_t^{MV}) less the cash that it owns ($Cash_t^{MV}$), relative to Berkshire's equity value ($Equity_t^{MV}$). We would like to compute the leverage using *market values* (which we indicate with the superscript *MV* in our notation), but for some variables we only observe *book values* (indicated with superscript *BV*) so we proceed as follows. We observe the market value of Berkshire's equity as the stock price multiplied by the shares outstanding and the cash holdings from Berkshire's consolidated balance sheet (see Appendix A). Further, the balance sheet also tells us the book value of the total assets (TA_t^{BV}) and the book value of equity ($Equity_t^{BV}$), which allows us to estimate the market value of the total asset (TA_t^{MV}) as

$$TA_t^{MV} = TA_t^{BV} + Equity_t^{MV} - Equity_t^{BV}$$

Based on this method, we estimate Buffett's average leverage to be 1.6-to-1. This indicates a non-trivial use of leverage. This magnitude of leverage can help explain why Berkshire realizes a high volatility despite investing in a number of relatively stable businesses.

By focusing on total assets to equity, we capture all kinds of liabilities and, as we discuss further below, Berkshire's financing arises from a variety of types of liabilities. The two main liabilities are debt and insurance float and, if we instead compute leverage as $(Equity_t^{MV} + Debt_t + Float_t)/Equity_t^{MV}$ then we estimate an average leverage of 1.4-to-1.

As another expression of Buffett's use of leverage, Berkshire's stock price is significantly more volatile than the portfolio of publicly traded stocks that it owns as we describe in Section 5, Table 2. In fact, Berkshire's 25% stock volatility is 1.4 times higher than the 17% volatility of the portfolio of public stocks, corresponding to a leverage of 1.4 assuming that Berkshire's private assets have similar volatility and ignoring diversification effects. This leverage number is similar to the leverage computed based on the balance sheet variables.

The magnitude of Buffett's leverage can partly explain how he outperforms the market, but only partly. If one applies 1.6-to-1 leverage to the market, that would magnify the market's average excess return to be about 10%, still falling far short of Berkshire's 19% average excess return.

In addition to considering the magnitude of Buffett's leverage, it is also interesting to consider his sources of leverage including their terms and costs. Berkshire's debt has benefitted from being highly rated, enjoying a AAA rating from 1989 to 2009. As an illustration of the low financing rates enjoyed by Buffett, Berkshire issued the first ever negative-coupon security in 2002, a senior note with a warrant.[5]

Berkshire's more anomalous cost of leverage, however, is due to its insurance float. Collecting insurance premia up front and later paying a diversified set of claims is like taking a "loan." Table 3 shows that the estimated average annual cost of Berkshire's insurance float is only 2.2%, more than 3 percentage points below the average T-bill rate. Hence, Buffett's low-cost insurance and reinsurance business have given him a significant advantage in terms of unique access to cheap, term leverage. We estimate that 36% of Berkshire's liabilities consist of insurance float on average.

Based on the balance sheet data, Berkshire also appears to finance part of its capital expenditure using tax deductions for accelerated depreciation of property, plant and equipment as provided for under the IRS rules. E.g., Berkshire reports $28 Billion of such deferred tax liabilities in 2011 (page 49 of the Annual Report). Accelerating depreciation is similar to an interest-free loan in the sense that (i) Berkshire enjoys a tax saving earlier than it otherwise would have, and (ii) the dollar amount of the tax when it is paid in the

---

[5] See http://www.berkshirehathaway.com/news/may2202.html

future is the same as the earlier savings (i.e. the tax liability does not accrue interest or compound).

Berkshire's remaining liabilities include accounts payable and derivative contract liabilities. Indeed, Berkshire has sold a number of derivative contracts, including writing index option contracts on several major equity indices, notably put options, and credit default obligations (see, e.g., the 2011 Annual Report). Berkshire states:

> *We received the premiums on these contracts in full at the contract inception dates ... With limited exceptions, our equity index put option and credit default contracts contain no collateral posting requirements with respect to changes in either the fair value or intrinsic value of the contracts and/or a downgrade of Berkshire's credit ratings.*
>
> *– Warren Buffett, Berkshire Hathaway Inc., Annual Report, 2011.*

Hence, Berkshire's sale of derivatives may both serve as a source of financing and as a source of revenue as such derivatives tend to be expensive (Frazzini and Pedersen (2012)). Frazzini and Pedersen (2012) show that investors that are either unable or unwilling to use leverage will pay a premium for instruments that embed the leverage, such as option contracts and levered ETFs. Hence, Buffett can profit by supplying this embedded leverage as he has a unique access to stable and cheap financing.

5. Decomposing Buffett: Public Stocks vs. Private Companies

Berkshire Hathaway stock return can be decomposed into the performance of the publicly traded companies that it owns, the performance of the privately held companies that it owns, and the leverage it uses. The performance of the publicly traded companies is a measure of Buffett's stock selection ability whereas the performance of the privately held companies additionally captures his success as a manager.

To evaluate Buffett's pure stock selection ability, we collect the portfolio of publicly held companies using Berkshire's 13F filings to the Securities and Exchange Commission, and we construct a monthly times series of the market value of all Berkshire's public stocks ($Public_t^{MV}$) as well as the monthly return on this mimicking portfolio (r_{t+1}^{public}). Specifically, at the end of each calendar quarter, we collect Berkshire's common stock holdings from its 13F filing and compute portfolio monthly returns, weighted by Berkshire's dollar holdings, under the assumption that the firm did not change holdings between reports. The stocks in the portfolio are refreshed quarterly based on the latest 13F, and the portfolio is rebalanced monthly to keep constant weights.

We cannot directly observe the value and performance of Buffett's private companies, but we can back them out based on what we do know. First, we can infer the market value of private holdings ($Private_t^{MV}$) as the residual given that we can observe the value of the total assets, the value of the publicly traded stocks, and the cash (see Buffett's balance sheet above):

$$Private_t^{MV} = TA_t^{MV} - Public_t^{MV} - Cash_t^{MV}$$

We then compute the return of these private holdings ($r_{t+1}^{Private}$) in a way that is immune to changes in the public stock portfolio and to splits/issuance using split-adjusted returns as follows:

$$r_{t+1}^{Private} = \frac{\Delta Private_{t+1}^{MV}}{Private_t^{MV}}$$

$$= \frac{r_{t+1}^f Liabilities_t^{MV} + r_{t+1}^{Equity} Equity_t^{MV} - r_{t+1}^{public} Public_t^{MV} - r_{t+1}^f Cash_t^{MV}}{Private_t^{MV}}$$

Here, r_{t+1}^f is the risk-free T-Bill return, r_{t+1}^{Equity} is the return on Berkshire's stock, and the market value of liabilities is estimated as $Liabilities_t^{MV} = TA_t^{MV} - Equity_t^{MV}$.

We note that our estimate of the value of Berkshire's private companies includes the value that the market attaches to Buffett himself (since it is based on the overall value of Berkshire Hathaway). To the extent that there is randomness or mispricing in Berkshire's stock price (e.g., due to the Buffett-specific element), the estimated value and return of the private companies may be noisy.

Given our estimates for Buffett's public and private returns as well as his leverage, we can decompose Berkshire's performance. (See the appendix for a rigorous derivation.) Berkshire's excess return can be decomposed into a weighted average of the return on the public stocks and the return of the private companies, leveraged up by L:

$$r_{t+1}^{Equity} - r_{t+1}^f = \left[w_t \left(r_{t+1}^{private} - r_{t+1}^f \right) + (1 - w_t) \left(r_{t+1}^{public} - r_{t+1}^f \right) \right] L_t$$

Berkshire's relative weight w_t on the private holdings is naturally given by

$$w_t = \frac{Private_t^{MV}}{Private_t^{MV} + Public_t^{MV}}$$

Empirically, we find that Berkshire owns 63% private companies on average from 1980 to 2011, the remaining 37% being invested in public stocks. Berkshire's reliance on private companies has been increasing steadily over time, from less than 20% in the early 1980s to more than 80% in 2011.

Table 2 shows the performance of both Buffett's public and private positions. We see that both perform relatively well. Both Buffett's public and private portfolios exceed the overall stock market in terms of average excess return, risk, and Sharpe ratio. We see that the public stocks have a higher Sharpe ratio than the private stocks, suggesting that Buffett's skill comes mostly from his ability to pick stocks, and not necessarily his value added as a manager.

Berkshire Hathaway's overall stock return is far above returns of both the private and public portfolios. This is because Berkshire is not just a weighted average of the public and private components. It is also leveraged, which magnifies returns. Further, Berkshire's Sharpe ratio is higher than those of the public and private parts, reflecting the benefits of diversification (and possibly benefits from time-varying leverage and time-varying public/private weights).

6. Buffett's Alpha and Investment Style: What Type of Stocks?

We have seen that Buffett's returns can be attributed to his stock selection and his ability to apply leverage, but how then does he pick his companies? To address this, we consider Buffett's factor exposures:

$$r_t - r_t^f = \alpha + \beta_1 MKT_t + \beta_2 SMB_t + \beta_3 HML_t + \beta_4 UMD_t + \beta_5 BAB_t + \beta_6 QMJ_t + \varepsilon_t$$

As seen in Table 4, we run this regression for the excess return $r_t - r_t^f$ of, respectively, Berkshire Hathaway stock, the portfolio of publicly held stocks inferred from the 13F filings, and the portfolio of private companies computed as described above.

For each of these returns, we first run a regression on the market return, MKT. Berkshire has a beta less than one and a significant alpha. We next control for the standard factors that capture the effects of size, value (Fama and French (1993)), and momentum (Asness (1994), Carhart (1997), Jegadeesh and Titman (1993)). The size factor small-minus-big (SMB) is a strategy of going long small stocks and short large stocks. Hence, a positive loading on SMB reflects a tendency to buy small stocks while Berkshire's negative loading reflects a tendency to buy large stocks. The value factor (HML) a strategy of buying high-book-to-market stocks while shortselling low-book-to-market stocks. Berkshire's positive loading therefore reflects a tendency of buying stocks that are cheap in the sense of having a high book value relative to their market value. The last of the four "standard" factors is the momentum factor UMD, which corresponds to buying stocks that have been "up" in the sense of outperforming the market, while shorting the stocks that are relatively "down". Berkshire's insignificant loading on *UMD* means that Buffett is not chasing trends in his stock selection.

Collectively, these four standard factors do not explain much of Buffett's alpha as seen in Table 4. Since Buffett's alpha cannot be explained by standard factors studied by academics, his success has to date been considered a sign of his unique skill or as a mystery.

Our innovation is to also control for the Betting Against Beta (*BAB*) factor of Frazzini and Pedersen (2013) as well as the quality factor (*QMJ*, "Quality Minus Junk") of Asness, Frazzini, and Pedersen (2013). A loading on the *BAB* factor reflects a tendency to buy safe (i.e., low-beta) stocks while shying away from risky (i.e., high-beta) stocks. Similarly, a loading on the quality *QMJ* factor reflects a tendency to buy high-quality companies, that is, companies that are profitable, growing, safe and have high payout (see Asness, Frazzini, and Pedersen (2013) for details).

We see that Berkshire loads significantly on the *BAB* and *QMJ* factors, reflecting that Buffett likes to buy safe, high-quality stocks. Controlling for these factors drives the alpha of Berkshire's public stock portfolio down to a statistically insignificant annualized 0.3%, meaning that these factors almost completely explain the performance of Buffett's public portfolio. Hence, a significant part of the secret behind Buffett's success is the fact that he buys safe, high-quality, value stocks. We also explain a large part of Berkshire's overall stock return and the private part in the sense that their alphas become statistically insignificant, although it is worth noting that the point estimate of Berkshire's alpha only drops by about half.

While Buffett is known as the ultimate value investor, we find that his focus on safe quality stocks may in fact be at least as important to his performance. Our statistical finding is consistent with Buffett's own words:

> *I could give you other personal examples of "bargain-purchase" folly but I'm sure you get the picture: It's far better to buy a wonderful company at a fair price than a fair company at a wonderful price.*
>
> *– Warren Buffett, Berkshire Hathaway Inc., Annual Report, 1989.*

We emphasize again that being able to explain Buffett's returns using factors from academic papers written decades after Buffett put them into practice does not make Buffett's success any less impressive. It is nevertheless interesting to discover the importance of leveraging low-beta, high-quality stocks for the person known as the "ultimate value investor."

7. A Systematic Buffett Strategy

Given that we can attribute Buffett's performance to leverage and his focus on safe, high-quality, value stocks, it is natural to consider how well we can do by implementing these investment themes in a systematic way. Whereas Buffett is known as an active stock picker, we will try to go back to Buffett's roots and, in the spirit of Graham and Dodd (1934), focus on systematically implemented screens.

We consider systematic Buffett-style portfolios that track Buffett's market exposure and active stock-selection themes. First, we capture Buffett's market exposure

$\beta^{Buffett}$ as the slope of a univariate regression of Berkshire's excess returns on the market portfolio. Second, we capture Buffett's stock selection tilts by running a regression of his monthly beta-adjusted returns on the factors that help explain his performance as described in Section 6:

$$r_t - r_t^f - \beta^{Buffett} MKT_t = \alpha + mMKT_t + sSMB_t + hHML_t + uUMD_t + bBAB_t + qQMJ_t + \varepsilon_t$$

The regression coefficients are equal to those in column 3 of Table 4 with the exception that the market loading is reduced by an amount equal to $\beta^{Buffett}$. The right-hand side excluding the alpha and the error term captures Buffett's *active* stock selection tilts:

$$r_t^A = m\, MKT_t + s\, SMB_t + h\, HML_t + u\, UMD_t + b\, BAB_t + q\, QMJ_t$$

We rescale this active return series to match Berkshire's idiosyncratic volatility σ_I to simulate the use of leverage and to counter any attenuation bias:

$$r_t^{Active} = r_t^A \frac{\sigma_I}{\sigma_{r_t^A}}$$

Finally, we add back Buffett's market exposure and the risk free return r_t^f to construct our systematic Buffett-style portfolio:

$$r_t^{Buffet\ style} = r_t^f + \beta^{Buffett}MKT_t + r_t^{Active}$$

Our systematic Buffett-style strategy is a diversified portfolio that matches Berkshire's beta, idiosyncratic volatility, total volatility, and relative active loadings.

We similarly construct a Buffett-style portfolio based on the loadings and volatility of Berkshire's public and private equity holdings. (These use the coefficients from columns 6 and 9 in Table 4). Table 2 reports the performance of our systematic Buffett-style portfolios and Figure 3 shows the cumulative return of Berkshire Hathaway, Buffett's public stocks and our systematic Buffett-style strategies. Finally, Table 5 reports correlations, alphas, and loadings for our systematic Buffett-style portfolios and their actual Buffett counterparts.

As seen in the tables and figures, the performance of the systematic Buffett-style portfolios are comparable to Buffett's actual return. Since the simulated Buffett-style portfolios do not account for transaction costs and other costs and benefit from hindsight, their apparent outperformance should be discounted. The main insight here is the high co-variation between Buffett's actual performance and the performance of a diversified Buffett-style strategy.

We match the public stock portfolio especially closely, perhaps because this public portfolio is observed directly and its returns are calculated based on public stocks returns using the same methodology as our systematic portfolios. Berkshire's overall stock price, on the other hand, may have idiosyncratic price variation (e.g., due to the value of Buffett himself) that cannot be replicated using other stocks. This idiosyncratic Berkshire variation is even more severe for the private part, which may also suffer from measurement issues.

The comparison between Berkshire's public stock portfolio and the corresponding Buffett-style portfolio is also the cleaner test of Buffett's stock selection since *both* are simulated returns without any transaction costs or taxes. Indeed, the correlation between our systematic portfolio and Berkshire's public stock portfolio (shown in Table 5) is 75%, meaning that our systematic portfolio explains 57% of the variance of the public stock portfolio. The correlations for the Berkshire's stock price and Buffett's private investments are lower (47% and 27% respectively), but still large in magnitude. Table 5 also shows that our systematic portfolios have significant alphas with respect to their corresponding Buffett counterpart, while none of the Buffett portfolios have statistically significant alphas with respect to their systematic counterpart. This may be because our systematic portfolios have similar factor tilts as Buffett's, but they hold a much larger number of securities, thus benefitting from diversification.

The Berkshire Hathaway stock return does reflect the incurred transaction costs and possibly additional taxes, so that makes Berkshire's performance all the more impressive. Given Berkshire's modest turnover, transaction costs were likely small initially. As Berkshire grew, so did transaction costs and this could potentially account for some of Berkshire's diminishing returns over time. Further, Berkshire may have been increasingly forced to focus on large stocks. Indeed, Table 4 shows that Berkshire has a negative loading on the size factor SMB, reflecting a tendency to buy large firms. However, Berkshire initially focused on small firms (reflected in a positive SMB loading in the first half of the time period, not shown), and only became biased towards large stocks in the later time period. Hence, Berkshire's diminishing returns could also be related to capacity constraints.

Assessing the impact of taxes on Berkshire's performance is complicated. For Berkshire's private holdings, the joint ownership in a multinational company is associated with tax advantages. For the public stocks, Berkshire could face double corporate taxes, that is, pay tax both indirectly in the portfolio companies' earnings and in Berkshire as it receives dividends or realizes capital gains. However, Berkshire can deduct 70-80% of the dividends received, defer capital gains taxes by holding on to the positions such that gains remain unrealized,[6] and minimize taxes by allocating earnings abroad as a multinational.[7] Hence, it is difficult to assess whether Berkshire is at a tax disadvantage overall.

In addition to the systematic long-short portfolios, we also compute a long-only, unleveraged systematic Buffett-style strategy. At the end of each calendar month, we sort securities based on the portfolio weights corresponding to our active tilts r_t^{Active} and construct an equal weighted portfolio that holds the top 50 stocks with the highest

---

[6] For a corporation, capital gains are subject to corporate taxes at 35% (and there is no special provision for long-term capital gains). While capital gains taxes can be deferred from a *cash-flow perspective* as long as they are unrealized, the accrued capital gains tax does nevertheless lead to an expense from a *GAAP-accounting perspective*. Said differently, Berkshire does not *pay* any taxes for unrealized capital gains, but such unrealized capital gains do lower Berkshire's reported *earnings* and hence its book value of equity, while raising the GAAP liability called principally deferred income taxes.

[7] For instance, Berkshire's 2011 Annual Report states: "We have not established deferred income taxes with respect to undistributed earnings of certain foreign subsidiaries. Earnings expected to remain reinvested indefinitely were approximately $6.6 billion as of December 31, 2011. Upon distribution as dividends or otherwise, such amounts would be subject to taxation in the U.S. as well as foreign countries. However, U.S. income tax liabilities would be offset, in whole or in part, by allowable tax credits with respect to income taxes previously paid to foreign jurisdictions. Further, repatriation of all earnings of foreign subsidiaries would be impracticable to the extent that such earnings represent capital needed to support normal business operations in those jurisdictions. As a result, we currently believe that any incremental U.S. income tax liabilities arising from the repatriation of distributable earnings of foreign subsidiaries would not be material."

portfolio weight. Table 2 shows that these simpler Buffett-style portfolios also perform well, albeit not as well as when we allow short selling.

As a final robustness check, we consider Buffett-style portfolios that do not rely on in-sample regression coefficients. Specifically, we create an implementable Buffett-style strategy by only using information up to month t to construct portfolio weights for the next month $t + 1$. As seen in Appendix C, these portfolios have very similar performance and alphas as our full sample Buffett-style portfolios.

In summary, if one had applied leverage to a portfolio of safe, high-quality, value stocks consistently over this time period, then one would have achieved a remarkable return, as did Buffett. Of course, he started doing it half a century before we wrote this paper!

8. Conclusion

We rigorously study Buffett's record, comparing it to the long-term performance of other stocks and mutual funds, and decomposing Buffett's performance into its components due to leverage, shares in publicly traded equity, and wholly-owned companies. We shed new light on the efficiency of capital markets in two ways: (i) by studying in a novel way the famous coin-flipping debate at the 1984 Columbia conference between Michael Jensen (representing the efficient market economists) and Warren Buffett (representing the people of Graham-and-Doddsville); and (ii) by showing how Buffett's record can be viewed as an expression of the practical implementability of academic factor returns after transaction costs and financing costs.

We document how Buffett's performance is outstanding as the best among all stocks and mutual funds that have existed for at least 30 years. Nevertheless, his Sharpe ratio of 0.76 might be lower than many investors imagine. While optimistic asset managers often claim to be able to achieve Sharpe ratios above 1 or 2, long-term investors might do well by setting a realistic performance goal and bracing themselves for the tough periods that even Buffett has experienced.

In essence, we find that the secret to Buffett's success is his preference for cheap, safe, high-quality stocks combined with his consistent use of leverage to magnify returns while surviving the inevitable large absolute and relative drawdowns this entails. Indeed, we find that stocks with the characteristics favored by Buffett have done well in general, that Buffett applies about 1.6-to-1 leverage financed partly using insurance float with a low financing rate, and that leveraging safe stocks can largely explain Buffett's performance.

Buffett has become the focal point of the intense debate about market efficiency among academics, practitioners, and in the media (see, e.g., Malkiel (2012)). The most recent Nobel prize has reignited this debate and, as a prototypical example, Forbes[8] writes "In the real world of investments, however, there are obvious arguments against the EMH. There are investors who have beaten the market – Warren Buffett." The efficient-market counter argument is that Buffett may just have been lucky. Our findings suggest that Buffett's success is not luck or chance, but reward for a successful implementation of exposure to factors that have historically produced high returns.

---

[8] Forbes (11/1/2013), "What is Market Efficiency."

At the same time, Buffett's success shows that the high returns of these academic factors are not just "paper returns", but these returns could be realized in the real world after transaction costs and funding costs, at least by Warren Buffett. Hence, to the extent that value and quality factors challenge the efficient market hypothesis, the actual returns of Warren Buffett strengthen this evidence. Further, Buffett's exposure to the BAB factor and his unique access to leverage are consistent with the idea that the BAB factor represents reward to the use of leverage.

References

Asness, C. S. (1994), "Variables that Explain Stock Returns", Ph.D. Dissertation, University of Chicago.

Asness, C., A. Frazzini, and L. H. Pedersen (2012a), "Leverage Aversion and Risk Parity", *Financial Analysts Journal*, 68(1), 47-59..

Asness, C., A. Frazzini, and L. H. Pedersen (2013), "Quality Minus Junk", working paper, AQR Capital Management, New York University.

Black, F. (1972), "Capital market equilibrium with restricted borrowing," *Journal of business*, 45, 3, pp. 444-455.

Black, F., M.C. Jensen, and M. Scholes (1972), "The Capital Asset Pricing Model: Some Empirical Tests." In Michael C. Jensen (ed.), Studies in the Theory of Capital Markets, New York, pp. 79-121.

Buffett, W.E. (1984), "The Superinvestors of Graham-and-Doddsville," Columbia Business School Magazine, 4-15.

Carhart, M. (1997), "On persistence in mutual fund performance", *Journal of Finance* 52, 57–82.

Fama, E.F. and French, K.R. (1993), "Common risk factors in the returns on stocks and bonds", *Journal of Financial Economics* 33, 3–56.

Frazzini, A. and L. H. Pedersen (2013), "Betting Against Beta", *Journal of Financial Economics*, Forthcoming.

Frazzini, A. and L. H. Pedersen (2012), "Embedded Leverage", working paper, AQR Capital Management, New York University.

Graham, B. and D. L. Dodd (1934), "Security Analysis," McGraw Hill.

Jegadeesh, N. and S. Titman (1993), "Returns to Buying Winners and Selling Losers: Implications for Stock Market Efficiency," *The Journal of Finance*, vol. 48, no. 1, pp. 65-91.

Kacperczyk, M., C. Sialm, and L. Zheng (2008), "Unobserved Actions of Mutual Funds," Review of Financial Studies, 21, 2379-2416.

Lowenstein, R. (2008), "Buffett The Biography," Duckworth Press, London, UK.

Malkiel, B.G. (2012), "A Random Walk Down Wall Street: The Time-Tested Strategy for Successful Investing," Tenth Edition, W. W. Norton & Company, New York, NY.

Martin, G.S. and J. Puthenpurackal (2008), "Imitation is the Sincerest Form of Flattery: Warren Buffett and Berkshire Hathaway," working paper American University.

Rosenberg, B., Kenneth R., and Ronald L. (1985), "Persuasive evidence of market inefficiency," Journal of Portfolio Management 11, 9–16.

Stattman, D. (1980), "Book values and stock returns," Chicago MBA: A Journal of Selected Papers 5, 25–45.

Appendix A: Decomposing Berkshire's Return

We start with the definition of private returns:

$$r_{t+1}^{Private} = \frac{r_{t+1}^{f} Liabilities_t^{MV} + r_{t+1}^{Equity} Equity_t^{MV} - r_{t+1}^{public} Public_t^{MV} - r_{t+1}^{f} Cash_t^{MV}}{Private_t^{MV}}$$

and re-arrange as follows:

$$r_{t+1}^{Equity}$$

$$= r_{t+1}^{Private} \frac{Private_t^{MV}}{Equity_t^{MV}} + r_{t+1}^{Public} \frac{Public_t^{MV}}{Equity_t^{MV}} - r_{t+1}^{f} \frac{Liabilities_t^{MV} - Cash_t^{MV}}{Equity_t^{MV}}$$

$$= \left(r_{t+1}^{private} \frac{Public_t^{MV}}{Private_t^{MV} + Public_t^{MV}} + r_{t+1}^{public} \frac{Public_t^{MV}}{Public_t^{MV} + Public_t^{MV}} \right) L_t$$

$$- r_{t+1}^{f} \frac{Liabilities_t^{MV} - Cash_t^{MV}}{Equity_t^{MV}}$$

where we use that

$$L_t = \frac{TA_t^{MV} - Cash_t^{MV}}{Equity_t^{MV}} = \frac{Private_t^{MV} + Public_t^{MV}}{Equity_t^{MV}}$$

The excess return of Berkshire can be written in terms of the weight of the private holdings,

$$w_t = \frac{Private_t^{MV}}{Private_t^{MV} + Public_t^{MV}}$$

as follows:

$$r_{t+1}^{Equity} - r_{t+1}^f = \left[w_t \, r_{t+1}^{private} + (1 - w_t) r_{t+1}^{public} \right] L_t$$
$$- r_{t+1}^f \left(\frac{Liabilities_t^{MV} - Cash_t^{MV}}{Equity_t^{MV}} + 1 \right)$$
$$= \left[w_t \left(r_{t+1}^{private} - r_{t+1}^f \right) + (1 - w_t) \left(r_{t+1}^{public} - r_{t+1}^f \right) \right] L_t$$
$$- r_{t+1}^f \left(\frac{Liabilities_t^{MV} - Cash_t^{MV}}{Equity_t^{MV}} + 1 - L_t \right)$$
$$= \left[w_t \left(r_{t+1}^{private} - r_{t+1}^f \right) + (1 - w_t) \left(r_{t+1}^{public} - r_{t+1}^f \right) \right] L_t$$

This equation shows precisely how we decompose Buffett's returns: The Berkshire equity excess return depends on the excess returns of private and public holdings, their relative importance, and the degree of leverage.

Note that our 13F holdings data and mimicking portfolio returns r_{t+1}^{public} start in 1980. However, our way of estimating returns from private holdings produce very noisy estimates for the first 3 years of the sample. There are several outliers in the imputed $r_{t+1}^{private}$ in the first years of the sample, with several returns exceeding +100% monthly. Therefore, we focus most of the analysis on $r_{t+1}^{private}$ on the period 1984 to 2011 where our method produces less noisy estimates.

Appendix B: Data Sources and Methodology

The data in this study are derived from a variety of sources.

Stock return data

Stock return and price data is from the CRSP database. Our data includes all domestic common stocks (share code 10 and 11) on the CRSP tape between December 1925 and December 2011. To compute Berkshire Hathaway's stock returns we value-weight both share classes A and B based on lagged market capitalization (Berkshire Hathaway introduced a share class B in April 1996). The stock return data for Berkshire Hathaway on the CRSP tape starts in 1976. Hence, we only have data on the last 35 years of Warren Buffett's record. He ran various private investment partnership from 1957 to 1969, started trading Berkshire Hathaway in 1962, took control of Berkshire in 1965, and started using Berkshire as his main investment vehicle after he closed his partnerships in 1969 (Lowenstein (2008)). At the time of writing we have been unable to collect data on Berkshire Hathaway's stock price prior to its introduction on the CRSP tape and Buffett's' partnership performance so our study covers the period 1976 to 2011, which can be viewed as a conservative estimate of Buffett's complete track record and out-of-sample evidence relative to his first almost 20 years of success.

Balance sheet data

Our main source of balance sheet data is the Compustat/XpressFeed database. However, due to the presence of several errors in the cash item (especially in the quarterly reports in the early part of the sample) we check and correct this data with information extracted from the original 10-K company filings as well as information from Berkshire's annual letter to the shareholders. Berkshire holds a significant amount of cash on its balance sheet, which we hand collect from Berkshire's Annual Report, Form 10K. We make the following adjustments: For the end of 1985, the official cash number includes a significant amount of cash set aside for the purchases of Capital Cities Communications and Scott Fetzer. Therefore, we use the pro forma consolidated balance sheet presented in note (18) on page 42 of the Annual Report. For the end of 1987, we use the restated cash figure mentioned in the 1988 Annual Report note 1(b) page 25. For other balance sheet items, we also focus on annual balance sheet data.

13F holdings data

We download holdings data for Berkshire Hathaway from Thomson Financial Institutional (13F) Holding Database which includes holdings of all US entities exercising investment discretion over $100 million, filed with the SEC. The data on Berkshire's public stock holdings run from 1980 to 2009.

Mutual fund data

We collect mutual fund returns from the CRSP Mutual Fund Database. The data run from 1976 to 2011. We focus our analysis on open-end actively managed domestic equity mutual funds. Our sample selection procedure follows that of Kacperzczyk, Sialm, and Zheng (2008), and we refer to their Appendix for details about the screens that were used and summary statistics of the data.

Appendix C: An Implementable Systematic Buffett Strategy

Table C1 and C2 report returns of implementable systematic Buffett-style portfolios. We construct systematic Buffett-style portfolios tracking Buffett's active bets and having similar market exposure. At the of each calendar month t we run a regression of monthly active (beta-adjusted) returns of Berkshire on a set of portfolios using data up to month $t-1$:

$$r - r^f - \beta MKT = \alpha + m\,MKT + s\,SMB + h\,HML + u\,UMD + b\,BAB + q\,QMJ + \varepsilon$$

Where β is the slope of a univariate regression of Buffett's excess returns on the market portfolio, also computed using data up to month t. The explanatory variables are the monthly returns of the standard value, size, and momentum factors as well as the BAB factor (Frazzini and Pedersen (2013)) and QMJ quality factor (Asness, Frazzini and Pedersen (2013)). To run the time-series regression, we require at least 60 monthly observations. The $t+1$ Buffett-style portfolio's active return r_{t+1}^{Active} is equal to the sum of the returns of the explanatory variables with portfolio weights equal to the regression coefficients rescaled to match the conditional active volatility of Berkshire's return:

$$\tilde{r}_{t+1}^A = m_t\,MKT_{t+1} + s_t\,SMB_{t+1} + h_t\,HML_{t+1} + u_t\,UMD_{t+1} + b_t\,BAB_{t+1} + q_t\,QMJ_{t+1}$$

$$r_{t+1}^{Active} = \tilde{r}_{t+1}^A \frac{\sigma_{t,I}}{\sigma_{t,\tilde{r}^A}}$$

where $\sigma_{t,I}$ is Berkshire's idiosyncratic volatility, estimated using data up to month t. Finally, we add back Buffett's market exposure

$$r_{t+1}^s = r^f + \beta_t MKT_{t+1} + r_{t+1}^{Active}$$

Note our notation, the subscript t indicates that quantities are known at portfolio formation date t. Our systematic Buffett-style return r_{t+1}^S corresponds to the return of a diversified self-financing long-short portfolio matching Berkshire's conditional beta, market-adjusted volatility and relative active loadings at portfolio formation. These portfolios use only information available in real-time. Table C1 and C2 show returns of Berkshire Hathaway, Berkshire's public stock holdings as well as our systematic Buffett-style strategy.

In addition to the systematic long-sort portfolios, we also compute a real-time long-only, unlevered systematic Buffett-style strategy. At the end of each calendar month t, we sort securities based on the portfolio weights corresponding to our active tilts computed using data up month t and construct an equal weighted portfolio that holds the top 50 stocks with the highest portfolio weight.

Table C1

Buffett's Return Decomposed into Leverage, Public Stocks, and Private Companies as well as the Performance of an Implementable Systematic Buffett Strategy.

This table reports average annual return in excess of the T-Bill rate, annualized volatility, Sharpe ratio, market beta, Information ratio, and sub-period returns. We report statistics for, respectively, Berkshire Hathaway stock, the mimicking portfolio of Berkshire's publicly traded stocks as reported in its 13F filings, the mimicking portfolio of Berkshire's private holdings, the CRSP value-weighted market return, and a systematic mimicking portfolio of Buffett's strategy. To construct the mimicking portfolio of Berkshire's publicly traded stocks, at the end of each calendar quarter, we collect Berkshire's common stock holdings from its 13F filings and compute portfolio monthly returns, weighted by Berkshire's dollar holdings, under the assumption that the firm did not change holdings between reports. The stocks in the portfolio are refreshed quarterly based on the latest 13F and the portfolio is rebalanced monthly to keep constant weights. The mimicking portfolio of Berkshire's private holdings is constructed following the procedure described Appendix A. The systematic Buffett-style portfolios are constructed from a regression of monthly excess returns. The explanatory variables are the monthly returns of the standard size, value, and momentum factors, the Frazzini and Pedersen (2013) Betting-Against-Beta factor, and the Asness, Frazzini and Pedersen (2013) Quality Minus Junk (QMJ) factor. The procedure is described in Appendix C. Returns, volatilities and Sharpe ratios are annualized. "Idiosyncratic volatility" is the volatility of residual of a regression of monthly excess returns on market excess returns.

	Buffett Performance				Buffett-Style Portfolio			Buffett-Style Portfolio Long Only		
	Berkshire Hathaway	Public U.S. stocks (from 13F filings)	Private holdings	Overall stock market performance	Berkshire Hathaway	Public U.S. stocks (from 13F filings)	Private holdings	Berkshire Hathaway	Public U.S. stocks (from 13F filings)	Private holdings
Sample	1976-2011	1980-2011	1984-2011	1976-2011	1981-2011	1985-2011	1988-2011	1981-2011	1985-2011	1988-2011
Beta	0.68	0.77	0.28	1.00	0.66	0.68	0.29	0.81	0.82	0.89
Average excess return	19.0%	11.8%	9.6%	6.1%	39.3%	19.3%	17.6%	9.4%	7.5%	9.2%
Total Volatility	24.8%	17.2%	22.3%	15.8%	30.9%	19.2%	28.7%	15.3%	15.4%	16.0%
Idiosyncratic Volatility	22.4%	12.0%	21.8%	0.0%	29.1%	15.8%	28.4%	8.5%	8.0%	8.2%
Sharpe ratio	0.76	0.69	0.43	0.39	1.27	1.01	0.61	0.62	0.49	0.58
Information ratio	0.66	0.56	0.36	0.00	1.20	0.95	0.56	0.49	0.49	0.47
Leverage	1.64	1.00	1.00	1.00	4.78	2.50	4.17			
Sub period excess returns:										
1976-1980	42.1%	31.4%		7.8%						
1981-1985	28.6%	20.9%	18.5%	4.3%	84.4%	42.2%		19.1%	27.4%	
1986-1990	17.3%	12.5%	9.7%	5.4%	30.8%	11.5%	36.9%	2.0%	3.1%	-0.6%
1991-1995	29.7%	18.8%	22.9%	12.0%	62.6%	34.7%	53.3%	20.9%	19.9%	20.2%
1996-2000	14.9%	12.0%	8.8%	11.8%	32.7%	22.2%	8.8%	10.5%	10.7%	13.8%
2001-2005	3.2%	2.2%	1.7%	1.6%	33.6%	20.9%	13.7%	5.8%	4.2%	5.8%
2006-2011	3.3%	3.0%	2.3%	0.7%	3.8%	5.6%	-9.3%	1.2%	-2.1%	2.1%

Table C1

Performance of Buffett and an Implementable Systematic Buffett-Style Portfolio

This table shows calendar-time portfolio returns. We report statistics for, respectively, Berkshire Hathaway stock, the mimicking portfolio of Berkshire's publicly traded stocks as reported in its 13F filings, the mimicking portfolio of Berkshire's private holdings, the CRSP value-weighted market return, and a systematic mimicking portfolio of Buffett's strategy. To construct the mimicking portfolio of Berkshire's publicly traded stocks, at the end of each calendar quarter, we collect Berkshire's common stock holdings from its 13F filings and compute portfolio monthly returns, weighted by Berkshire's dollar holdings, under the assumption that the firm did not change holdings between reports. The stocks in the portfolio are refreshed quarterly based on the latest 13F and the portfolio is rebalanced monthly to keep constant weights. The mimicking portfolio of Berkshire's private holdings is constructed following the procedure described Appendix A. The systematic Buffett-style portfolios are constructed from a regression of monthly excess returns. The explanatory variables are the monthly returns of the standard size, value, and momentum factors, the Frazzini and Pedersen (2013) Betting-Against-Beta factor, and the Asness, Frazzini and Pedersen (2013) Quality Minus Junk (QMJ) factor. The procedure is described in Appendix C. Alpha is the intercept in a regression of monthly excess return. Alphas are annualized, t-statistics are shown below the coefficient estimates, and 5% statistical significance is indicated in bold.

| | Regress Berkshire on Systematic Portfolio | | | Regress Systematic Portoflio on Berkshire | | |
	Berkshire Hathaway	Public U.S. stocks (from 13F filings)	Private holdings	Berkshire Hathaway	Public U.S. stocks (from 13F filings)	Private holdings
Sample	1976-2011	1980-2011	1984-2011	1976-2011	1980-2011	1984-2011
Alpha	3.7%	-0.6%	6.4%	**30.4%**	**12.1%**	**15.5%**
	(0.88)	-(0.21)	(1.61)	(5.81)	(4.11)	(2.58)
Loading	**0.32**	**0.56**	**0.11**	**0.55**	**0.70**	**0.26**
	(8.73)	(14.34)	(2.87)	(8.73)	(14.34)	(2.87)
Correlation	0.42	0.63	0.17	0.42	0.63	0.17
R2 bar	0.17	0.39	0.03	0.17	0.39	0.03

Tables and Figures

Table 1

Buffett's Performance Relative to All Other Stocks and Mutual Funds.

This table shows the Sharpe ratio (SR) and Information ratio (IR) of Berkshire Hathaway relative to the universe of common stocks on the CRSP Stock database from 1926 to 2011, and relative to the universe of actively managed equity mutual funds on the CRSP Mutual Fund database from 1976 to 2011. The Information ratio is defined as the intercept in a regression of monthly excess returns divided by the standard deviation of the residuals. The explanatory variable in the regression is the monthly excess returns of the CRSP value-weighted market portfolio. Sharpe ratios and information ratios are annualized.

	Sample Distribution of Sharpe Ratios					Buffett Performance	
Panel A: SR of Equity Mutual Funds	Number of stocks/funds	Median	95th Percentile	99th Percentile	Maximum	Rank	Percentile
All funds in CRSP data 1976 - 2011	3,479	0.242	0.49	1.09	2.99	88	97.5%
All funds alive in 1976 and 2011	140	0.37	0.52	0.76	0.76	1	100.0%
All funds alive in 1976 with at least 10-year history	264	0.35	0.51	0.65	0.76	1	100.0%
All funds with at least 10-year history	1,994	0.30	0.47	0.65	0.90	4	99.8%
All funds with at least 30-year history	196	0.37	0.51	0.72	0.76	1	100.0%
Panel B: SR of Common Stocks							
All stocks in CRSP data 1926 - 2011	23,390	0.195	0.61	1.45	2.68	1360	93.9%
All stocks alive in 1976 and 2011	598	0.32	0.44	0.56	0.76	1	100.0%
All stocks alive in 1976 with at least 10-year history	3,633	0.27	0.45	0.61	0.86	7	99.8%
All stocks with at least 10-year history	9,035	0.26	0.48	0.73	1.12	62	99.3%
All stocks with at least 30-year history	1,777	0.31	0.44	0.57	0.76	1	100.0%

	Sample Distribution of Information Ratios					Buffett Performance	
Panel C: IR of Equity Mutual Funds	Number of stocks/funds	Median	95th Percentile	99th Percentile	Maximum	Rank	Percentile
All funds in CRSP data 1976 - 2011	3,479	-0.060	0.39	0.89	2.84	100	97.1%
All funds alive in 1976 and 2011	140	0.050	0.39	0.68	0.81	2	99.3%
All funds alive in 1976 with at least 10-year history	264	-0.025	0.30	0.60	0.81	2	99.6%
All funds with at least 10-year history	1,994	0.022	0.38	0.77	1.22	42	97.9%
All funds with at least 30-year history	196	0.034	0.34	0.66	0.81	2	99.5%
Panel D: IR of Common Stocks							
All stocks in CRSP data 1926 - 2011	23,390	0.089	0.54	1.41	2.91	1510	93.3%
All stocks alive in 1976 and 2011	598	0.183	0.32	0.46	0.66	1	100.0%
All stocks alive in 1976 with at least 10-year history	3,633	0.146	0.36	0.57	0.80	13	99.7%
All stocks with at least 10-year history	9,035	0.136	0.38	0.62	1.07	58	99.4%
All stocks with at least 30-year history	1,777	0.130	0.29	0.43	0.66	1	100.0%

Table 2
Buffett's Return Decomposed into Leverage, Public Stocks, and Private Companies as well as the Performance of a Systematic Buffett Strategy.

This table reports average annual return in excess of the T-Bill rate, annualized volatility, market beta, Information ratio, and sub-period returns. We report statistics for, respectively, Berkshire Hathaway stock, the mimicking portfolio of Berkshire's publicly traded stocks as reported in its 13F filings, the mimicking portfolio of Berkshire's private holdings, and a systematic mimicking portfolio of Buffett's strategy. To construct the mimicking portfolio of Berkshire's private holdings, the CRSP value-weighted market return, and a systematic mimicking portfolio of Buffett's strategy. To construct the mimicking portfolio of Berkshire's publicly traded stocks, at the end of each calendar quarter, we collect Berkshire's common stock holdings from its 13F filings and compute portfolio monthly returns, weighted by Berkshire's dollar holdings, under the assumption that the firm did not change holdings between reports. The stocks in the portfolio are refreshed quarterly based on the latest 13F and the portfolio is rebalanced monthly to keep constant weights. The mimicking portfolio of Berkshire's private holdings is constructed following the procedure described Appendix A. The systematic Buffett-style portfolios are constructed from a regression of monthly excess returns. The explanatory variables are the monthly returns of the standard size, value, and momentum factors, the Frazzini and Pedersen (2013) Betting-Against-Beta factor, and the Asness, Frazzini and Pedersen (2013) Quality Minus Junk (QMJ) factor. The procedure is described in Section 7. Returns, volatilities and Sharpe ratios are annualized. "Idiosyncratic volatility" is the volatility of residual of a regression of monthly excess returns on market excess returns.

	Buffett Performance				Buffett-Style Portfolio			Buffett-Style Portfolio Long Only		
Sample	Berkshire Hathaway	Public U.S. stocks (from 13F filings)	Private holdings	Overall stock market performance	Berkshire Hathaway	Public U.S. stocks (from 13F filings)	Private holdings	Berkshire Hathaway	Public U.S. stocks (from 13F filings)	Private holdings
	1976–2011	1980–2011	1984–2011	1976–2011	1976–2011	1980–2011	1984–2011	1976–2011	1980–2011	1984–2011
Beta	0.68	0.77	0.28	1.00	0.68	0.77	0.28	0.83	0.82	0.86
Average excess return	19.0%	11.8%	9.6%	6.1%	28.2%	19.3%	14.0%	7.0%	7.9%	7.4%
Total Volatility	24.8%	17.2%	22.3%	15.8%	24.8%	17.2%	22.3%	15.5%	15.1%	15.5%
Idiosyncratic Volatility	22.4%	12.0%	21.8%	0.0%	22.4%	12.0%	21.8%	8.2%	7.7%	7.5%
Sharpe ratio	0.76	0.69	0.43	0.39	1.14	1.13	0.63	0.45	0.52	0.48
Information ratio	0.66	0.56	0.36	0.00	1.07	1.18	0.56	0.24	0.52	0.28
Leverage	1.64	1.00	1.00	1.00	3.73	2.19	3.14			
Sub period excess returns:										
1976-1980	42.1%			7.8%	10.2%			4.6%		
1981-1985	28.6%	20.9%	18.5%	4.3%	54.8%	30.9%	35.9%	10.5%	13.4%	7.4%
1986-1990	17.3%	12.5%	9.7%	5.4%	23.7%	14.2%	16.0%	2.1%	4.4%	3.5%
1991-1995	29.7%	18.8%	22.9%	12.0%	38.5%	24.1%	24.5%	18.5%	19.0%	18.1%
1996-2000	14.9%	12.0%	8.8%	11.8%	33.2%	22.8%	17.4%	9.2%	9.2%	8.8%
2001-2005	3.2%	2.2%	1.7%	1.6%	33.0%	18.6%	14.1%	4.0%	4.9%	5.7%
2006-2011	3.3%	3.0%	2.3%	0.7%	4.7%	6.1%	-7.5%	0.6%	-0.4%	2.3%

Table 3

Buffett's Cost of Leverage: The Case of His Insurance Float

This table shows the cost of Berkshire's funds coming from insurance float. The data is hand-collected from Buffett's comment in Berkshire Hathaway's annual reports. Rates are annualized, in percent. * In years when cost of funds is reported as "less than zero" and no numerical value is available we set cost of funds to zero.

	Fraction of years with negative cost	Average cost of funds (Trucated)*	Spread over benckmark rates				
			T-Bill	Fed Funds rate	1-Month Libor	6-Month Libor	10-Year Bond
1976-1980	0.79	1.67	-4.59	-5.65			-5.76
1981-1985	0.20	10.95	1.10	-0.27			-1.28
1986-1990	0.00	3.07	-3.56	-4.61	-4.80	-4.90	-5.30
1991-1995	0.60	2.21	-2.00	-2.24	-2.46	-2.71	-4.64
1996-2000	0.60	2.36	-2.70	-3.10	-3.33	-3.48	-3.56
2001-2005	0.60	1.29	-0.82	-0.96	-1.05	-1.19	-3.11
2006-2011	1.00	-4.00	-5.84	-6.06	-6.29	-6.59	-7.67
Full sample	0.60	2.20	-3.09	-3.81	-3.69	-3.88	-4.80

Table 4

Buffett's Exposures: What Kind of Companies does Berkshire Own?

This table shows calendar-time portfolio returns. We report statistics for, respectively, Berkshire Hathaway stock, the mimicking portfolio of Berkshire's publicly traded stocks as reported in its 13F filings and the mimicking portfolio of Berkshire's private holdings. To construct the mimicking portfolio of Berkshire's publicly traded stocks, at the end of each calendar quarter, we collect Berkshire's common stock holdings from its 13F filings and compute portfolio monthly returns, weighted by Berkshire's dollar holdings, under the assumption that the firm did not change holdings between reports. The stocks in the portfolio are refreshed quarterly based on the latest 13F and the portfolio is rebalanced monthly to keep constant weights. The mimicking portfolio of Berkshire's private holdings is constructed following the procedure described in Appendix A. Alpha is the intercept in a regression of monthly excess return. The explanatory variables are the monthly returns of the standard size, value, and momentum factors, the Frazzini and Pedersen (2013) Betting-Against-Beta factor, and the Asness, Frazzini and Pedersen (2013) Quality Minus Junk (QMJ) factor. Alphas are annualized, t-statistics are shown below the coefficient estimates, and 5% statistical significance is indicated in bold.

	Berkshire stock 1976 - 2011			13F portfolio 1980 - 2011			Private Holdings 1984 - 20011		
Alpha	**12.1%**	**9.2%**	6.3%	**5.3%**	3.5%	0.3%	5.6%	4.6%	4.9%
	(3.19)	(2.42)	(1.58)	(2.53)	(1.65)	(0.12)	(1.35)	(1.08)	(1.09)
MKT	**0.84**	**0.83**	**0.95**	**0.86**	**0.86**	**0.98**	**0.40**	**0.40**	**0.39**
	(11.65)	(11.70)	(10.98)	(21.55)	(21.91)	(20.99)	(5.01)	(5.01)	(3.94)
SMB	**-0.32**	**-0.32**	-0.15	**-0.18**	**-0.18**	0.00	**-0.29**	**-0.29**	**-0.31**
	-(3.05)	-(3.13)	-(1.15)	-(3.14)	-(3.22)	(0.02)	-(2.59)	-(2.53)	-(2.17)
HML	**0.63**	**0.38**	**0.46**	**0.39**	**0.24**	**0.31**	**0.39**	0.28	0.27
	(5.35)	(2.79)	(3.28)	(6.12)	(3.26)	(4.24)	(3.07)	(1.89)	(1.81)
UMD	0.06	-0.03	-0.05	-0.02	**-0.08**	**-0.10**	0.09	0.04	0.05
	(0.90)	-(0.40)	-(0.71)	-(0.55)	-(1.98)	-(2.66)	(1.13)	(0.52)	(0.55)
BAB		**0.37**	**0.29**		**0.22**	**0.15**		0.16	0.17
		(3.61)	(2.67)		(4.05)	(2.58)		(1.40)	(1.41)
QMJ			**0.43**			**0.44**			-0.05
			(2.34)			(4.55)			-(0.24)
R2 bar	0.25	0.27	0.28	0.57	0.58	0.60	0.08	0.08	0.08

Table 5

Buffett's Returns Versus a Systematic Buffett Strategy

This table shows calendar-time portfolio returns. We report statistics for, respectively, Berkshire Hathaway stock, the mimicking portfolio of Berkshire's publicly traded stocks as reported in its 13F filings, the mimicking portfolio of Berkshire's private holdings, the CRSP value-weighted market return, and a systematic mimicking portfolio of Buffett's strategy. To construct the mimicking portfolio of Berkshire's publicly traded stocks, at the end of each calendar quarter, we collect Berkshire's common stock holdings from its 13F filings and compute portfolio monthly returns, weighted by Berkshire's dollar holdings, under the assumption that the firm did not change holdings between reports. The stocks in the portfolio are refreshed quarterly based on the latest 13F and the portfolio is rebalanced monthly to keep constant weights. The mimicking portfolio of Berkshire's private holdings is constructed following the procedure described Appendix A. The systematic Buffett-style portfolios are constructed from a regression of monthly excess returns. The explanatory variables are the monthly returns of the standard size, value, and momentum factors, the Frazzini and Pedersen (2013) Betting-Against-Beta factor, and the Asness, Frazzini and Pedersen (2013) Quality Minus Junk (QMJ) factor. The procedure is described in Section 7. Alpha is the intercept in a regression of monthly excess return. Alphas are annualized, t-statistics are shown below the coefficient estimates, and 5% statistical significance is indicated in bold.

| | Regress Berkshire on Systematic Portfolio | | | Regress Systematic Portoflio on Berkshire | | |
	Berkshire Hathaway	Public U.S. stocks (from 13F filings)	Private holdings	Berkshire Hathaway	Public U.S. stocks (from 13F filings)	Private holdings
Sample	1976-2011	1980-2011	1984-2011	1976-2011	1980-2011	1984-2011
Alpha	5.6%	-2.3%	5.8%	**19.3%**	**10.7%**	**11.4%**
	(1.44)	-(1.05)	(1.40)	(5.07)	(5.00)	(2.78)
Loading	**0.47**	**0.73**	**0.27**	**0.47**	**0.73**	**0.27**
	(10.97)	(20.83)	(5.08)	(10.97)	(20.83)	(5.08)
Correlation	0.47	0.73	0.27	0.47	0.73	0.27
R2 bar	0.22	0.53	0.07	0.22	0.53	0.07

Figure 1

How Berkshire Stacks Up in the Mutual Fund Universe.

This figure shows the distribution of annualized Information Ratios of all actively managed equity funds on the CRSP mutual fund database with at least 30 years of return history. Information ratio is defined as the intercept in a regression of monthly excess returns divided by the standard deviation of the residuals. The explanatory variable in the regression is the monthly excess returns of the CRSP value-weighted market portfolio. The vertical line shows the Information ratio of Berkshire Hathaway.

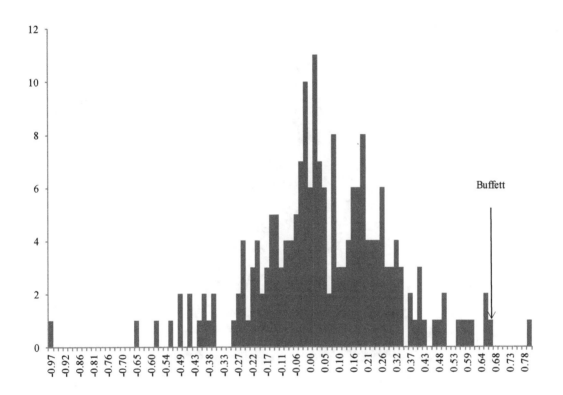

Figure 2

How Berkshire Stacks Up in the Common Stocks Universe.

This figure shows the distribution of annualized Information Ratios of all common stock on the CRSP database with at least 30 years of return history. Information ratio is defined as the intercept in a regression of monthly excess returns divided by the standard deviation of the residuals. The explanatory variable in the regression is the monthly excess returns of the CRSP value-weighted market portfolio. The vertical line shows the Information ratio of Berkshire Hathaway.

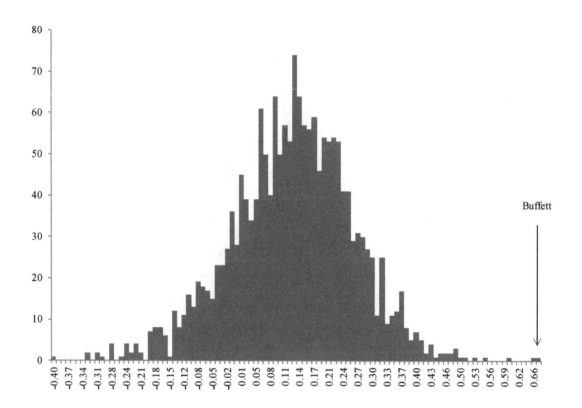

Figure 3

Performance of Buffett and Systematic Buffett-Style Portfolio.

Panel A of this figure shows the cumulative return of Berkshire Hathaway's portfolio of publicly traded stocks (as reported in its 13F filings), a corresponding systematic Buffett-mimicking portfolio, and the CRSP value-weighted market return (leveraged to the same volatility as Berkshire's public stocks). Similarly, Panel B shows the cumulative return of Berkshire Hathaway, a corresponding systematic Buffett-mimicking portfolio, and the CRSP value-weighted market return (leveraged to the same volatility as Berkshire). The systematic Buffett-style strategy is constructed from a regression of monthly excess returns (columns 3 and 6, respectively, in Table 4). The explanatory variables are the monthly returns of the standard market, size, value, and momentum factors as well as the Quality Minus Junk (QMJ) factor of Asness, Frazzini, and Pedersen (20134) and the *BAB* factor of Frazzini and Pedersen (2013). The systematic Buffett-style portfolio excess return is the sum of the explanatory variables multiplied by the respective regression coefficients, rescaled to match the volatility of Berkshire's return.

Panel A: Berkshire's Public Stocks and Buffett-Style Portfolio

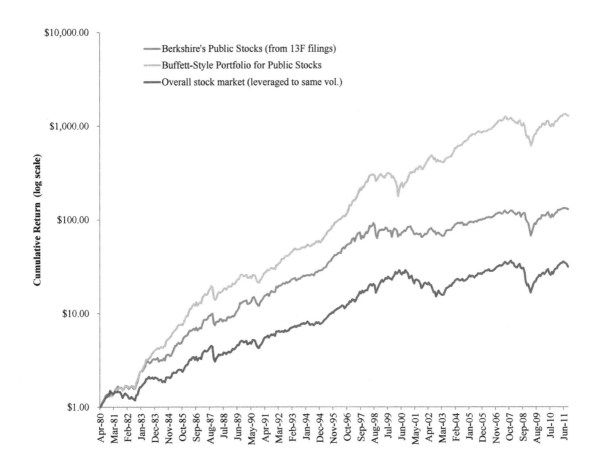

Figure 3 (continued)

Panel B: Berkshire Hathaway and Buffett-Style Portfolio

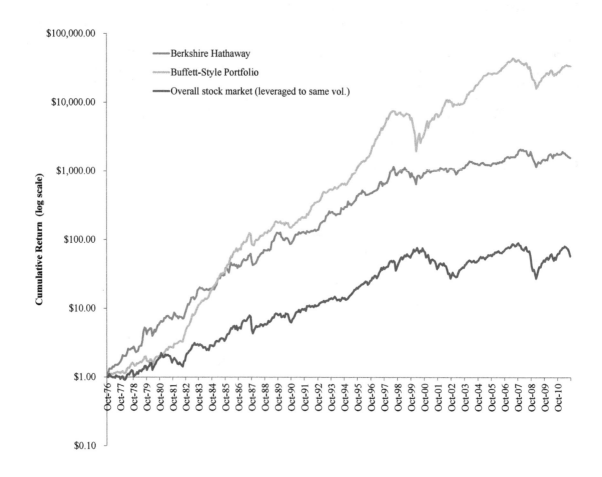